Greenland 2050: Navigating a Post-Global Warming Future

Greenland 2050: Navigating a Post-Global Warming Future
By Roberto Miguel Rodriguez
Chapter 1: The Future of Greenland After Global Warming
Understanding Climate Change and its Impact on Greenland

Climate change is a global phenomenon that has far-reaching implications for our planet, and few places are feeling its effects as acutely as Greenland. As the world grapples with the consequences of global warming, ecologists, politicians, journalists, educators, and the public must understand the specific challenges facing Greenland and its people.

Greenland, the world's largest island, is home to a fragile ecosystem that is highly vulnerable to climate change. Rising temperatures are causing rapid and widespread melting of the island's ice sheet, leading to rising sea levels and increased coastal erosion. This not only threatens the unique biodiversity of Greenland but also has significant implications for the global climate system.

One of the critical areas of concern is the future of Greenland after global warming. With the loss of its ice cover, new opportunities and challenges arise. The book explores the potential for sustainable tourism in post-global warming Greenland, highlighting the need for responsible practices that minimize environmental impact while showcasing the island's natural beauty.

Additionally, the book delves into the importance of renewable energy sources and infrastructure development in Greenland. As the region transitions away from fossil fuels, there is immense potential for harnessing the power of wind, solar, and hydroelectric energy. The book examines the role of these renewable sources in ensuring a sustainable future for Greenland and its people.

Adaptation and resilience strategies for Greenlandic communities are also explored as they face the reality of a warmer future. This includes the need for improved infrastructure, emergency response systems, and community engagement to ensure the well-being of the population in the face of changing climatic conditions.

Conservation and management of Greenland's unique ecosystems and biodiversity are also addressed. Efforts to protect and restore fragile habitats, as well as the preservation of traditional knowledge and practices, are crucial for maintaining the island's rich natural heritage.

The book also delves into the economic opportunities and challenges in a post-global warming Greenland. As new shipping routes open up and resource extraction becomes more feasible, there is a delicate balance to strike between economic development and environmental sustainability.

Furthermore, the book explores the impact of climate change on Greenlandic culture, language, and identity. As traditional ways of life are disrupted, it is essential to understand and address the social and cultural consequences of a warmer future.

Lastly, the book delves into the international cooperation and governance required for the future of Greenland after global warming. As climate change knows no borders, collaboration between nations is essential in addressing the challenges facing Greenland and ensuring a sustainable and prosperous future.

In conclusion, understanding climate change and its impact on Greenland is of paramount importance for ecologists, politicians, journalists, educators, and the public. This subchapter provides a comprehensive overview of the various aspects that need to be considered in navigating a post-global warming future for Greenland. By addressing the end of Greenland after global warming, sustainable tourism, renewable energy, adaptation strategies, conservation efforts, economic opportunities, cultural implications, and international cooperation, the book aims to equip readers with the knowledge and understanding needed to tackle the challenges ahead.

Greenland's Changing Environment: Rising Temperatures and Melting Ice

As the global climate continues to warm, Greenland's environment is undergoing significant transformations. Rising temperatures and melting ice are already having profound effects on this vast Arctic island. In this subchapter, we will explore the various dimensions of Greenland's changing environment and the implications for different stakeholders.

To begin, ecologists are closely monitoring the impact of rising temperatures on Greenland's unique ecosystems and biodiversity. The melting ice is altering the delicate balance of these ecosystems, affecting wildlife habitats and migration patterns. Researchers and policymakers must understand these changes to develop effective conservation and management strategies.

Politicians and journalists play a crucial role in raising awareness about Greenland's future after global warming. They must engage in informed discussions on sustainable tourism and renewable energy sources. Sustainable tourism in post-global warming Greenland can provide economic opportunities while preserving the fragile environment. Simultaneously, renewable energy sources and infrastructure development are vital for reducing greenhouse gas emissions and achieving a sustainable future.

Educators have the responsibility to educate the public about the impacts of climate change on Greenland. They can promote adaptation and resilience strategies for Greenlandic communities in a warmer future. These strategies may include developing new agricultural practices, enhancing infrastructure resilience, and ensuring access to clean water.

The changing environment also raises questions about the extraction of potential resources in Greenland. Melting ice may uncover valuable mineral deposits, but the extraction must be done responsibly to minimize environmental damage. Indigenous knowledge and traditional practices can provide valuable insights into resource management in a changing Greenlandic landscape.

The economic opportunities and challenges in post-global warming Greenland need to be carefully considered. The new Arctic shipping routes may open up trade implications, allowing Greenland to become a crucial hub for international commerce. However, it is essential to balance economic growth with environmental conservation and the preservation of Greenlandic culture and identity.

International cooperation and governance are vital for shaping the future of Greenland. Collaborative efforts are necessary to address the challenges posed by climate change effectively. This requires engaging with indigenous communities, incorporating their perspectives, and respecting their rights.

In conclusion, Greenland's changing environment presents a range of complex issues that require the collective efforts of ecologists, politicians, journalists, educators, and the public. By understanding the implications of rising temperatures and melting ice, we can navigate a post-global warming future for Greenland that is sustainable and resilient and respects the unique culture and ecosystems of this Arctic nation.

Chapter 2: Sustainable Tourism in Greenland After Global Warming

The Importance of Tourism for Greenland's Economy

Tourism plays a crucial role in the economy of Greenland, particularly in the context of a post-global warming future. As the effects of climate change continue to transform the country's landscape, the tourism industry offers both economic opportunities and challenges for Greenland. This subchapter will explore the significance of tourism for the country's economy, focusing on its potential to drive sustainable development, create employment, and promote cultural preservation.

With the melting of ice and the opening up of new landscapes, Greenland is becoming an increasingly attractive destination for tourists seeking unique experiences and untouched natural beauty. The country's majestic glaciers, fjords, and wildlife provide an unparalleled setting for adventure tourism, nature-based activities, and cultural exploration. As a result, tourism has the potential to become one of the leading sectors in Greenland's post-global warming economy.

Sustainable tourism is vital to ensuring the long-term viability of the industry and the preservation of Greenland's fragile ecosystems. By adopting responsible practices, such as promoting low-impact tourism, supporting local communities, and respecting indigenous knowledge and traditional methods, Greenland can capitalize on its natural and cultural assets without compromising their integrity. This approach not only safeguards the environment but also enhances the visitor experience and fosters a sense of authenticity.

Furthermore, tourism has the power to create employment opportunities for local communities, particularly in remote regions where alternative economic activities are scarce. By investing in training and capacity building, Greenland can empower its residents to become active participants in the tourism industry, benefiting from the revenue generated by visitor spending. Additionally, tourism-related infrastructure development, such as accommodations, transportation, and visitor centers, can stimulate economic growth and improve the quality of life for residents.

However, the rise of tourism also raises concerns about the potential impacts on Greenlandic culture, language, and identity. It is crucial to strike a balance between meeting the demands of tourists and preserving the unique cultural heritage of the indigenous communities. By integrating indigenous knowledge and traditional practices into tourism activities, Greenland can showcase its rich cultural tapestry while ensuring that local traditions and values are respected and upheld.

In conclusion, tourism holds excellent potential for Greenland's economy in a post-global warming future. By embracing sustainable practices, investing in local communities, and preserving cultural heritage, Greenland can harness the economic benefits of tourism while safeguarding its unique ecosystems and identity. However, careful planning, collaboration, and international cooperation will be essential to ensure that tourism contributes to a prosperous and resilient future for Greenland.

Sustainable Tourism Practices in a Warmer Greenland

As Greenland faces the challenges of a warmer future, it is essential to consider sustainable tourism practices that can ensure the preservation of its unique landscapes and cultural heritage. With the increasing interest in this Arctic country, it is crucial to strike a balance between economic development and environmental conservation. This subchapter aims to explore the potential strategies and initiatives that can be implemented to achieve sustainable tourism in post-global warming Greenland.

One of the critical aspects of sustainable tourism in Greenland is the promotion of renewable energy sources and infrastructure development. By investing in clean energy technologies such as wind and solar power, the tourism industry can reduce its carbon footprint and contribute to mitigating climate change. Additionally, the development of eco-friendly infrastructure, including sustainable accommodations and transportation systems, can further enhance the sustainability of tourism in the region.

Adaptation and resilience strategies for Greenlandic communities are also paramount in ensuring the long-term sustainability of tourism. As the environment changes, it is crucial to support local communities in adapting to the new conditions. This can involve providing training and resources for alternative livelihoods, promoting cultural preservation, and enhancing community resilience to climate-related challenges. By empowering local communities, tourism can become a catalyst for sustainable development and economic growth.

Conservation and management of Greenland's unique ecosystems and biodiversity should be a top priority in sustainable tourism practices. Strict regulations and guidelines need to be implemented to protect fragile ecosystems, wildlife, and cultural heritage sites. By working closely with scientists, indigenous communities, and conservation organizations, tourism operators can ensure that their activities have minimal impact on the environment and contribute to the preservation of Greenland's natural treasures.

Furthermore, sustainable tourism should also consider the impacts on Greenlandic culture, language, and identity. As the environment changes, so does the way of life for indigenous communities. It is essential to promote the preservation of traditional practices and knowledge, as they are integral to the cultural fabric of Greenland. By incorporating indigenous perspectives and practices into tourism experiences, visitors can gain a deeper understanding and appreciation for the local culture.

International cooperation and governance play a crucial role in shaping the future of Greenland after global warming. Collaboration between governments, organizations, and stakeholders can lead to the development of sustainable tourism policies and regulations. Additionally, partnerships with international organizations can provide funding and expertise to support sustainable tourism initiatives in Greenland.

In conclusion, sustainable tourism practices in a warmer Greenland are essential to ensure the preservation of its unique landscapes, biodiversity, and cultural heritage. By promoting renewable energy sources, supporting local communities, conserving ecosystems, and incorporating indigenous knowledge, tourism can play a pivotal role in driving sustainable development in the region. However, achieving this requires international cooperation, strong governance, and a commitment from all stakeholders involved. Only through these collective efforts can we navigate a post-global warming future for Greenland that is both economically prosperous and environmentally sustainable.

Chapter 3: Renewable Energy Sources and Infrastructure Development in Greenland

Harnessing Greenland's Renewable Energy Potential

Greenland, the world's largest island, is poised to become a leading force in renewable energy. As global warming continues to reshape the Arctic landscape, this subchapter explores the possibilities and challenges of harnessing Greenland's vast renewable energy potential.

With its abundance of natural resources, including hydroelectric power, wind energy, and geothermal sources, Greenland has the opportunity to transition to a sustainable energy future. This shift towards renewable energy is not only essential for mitigating climate change but also for ensuring the long-term viability of the island's communities and ecosystems.

To fully tap into Greenland's renewable energy potential, significant infrastructure development is required. The construction of hydroelectric dams, wind farms, and geothermal power plants will create jobs and stimulate economic growth. Moreover, this investment in sustainable infrastructure will help reduce the island's dependence on imported fossil fuels, making Greenland more self-sufficient and resilient in a post-global warming era.

The transition to renewable energy in Greenland also presents unique challenges. The harsh Arctic climate and remote location necessitate innovative technologies and engineering solutions. Researchers and engineers must develop energy systems that can withstand extreme weather conditions and operate efficiently in isolated areas. Additionally, partnerships with international experts and organizations will be crucial to access the necessary expertise and funding for renewable energy projects.

This subchapter also explores the potential impacts of renewable energy development on Greenlandic communities and ecosystems. While the transition to renewable energy brings economic opportunities, it must be managed carefully to avoid negative social and environmental consequences. Indigenous knowledge and traditional practices should be integrated into renewable energy projects, ensuring that Greenlandic culture, language, and identity are preserved and respected.

Furthermore, the development of renewable energy infrastructure opens up new possibilities for Arctic shipping routes and international trade. As ice continues to melt, previously impassable routes become navigable, connecting Greenland to global markets. This presents economic opportunities but also requires international cooperation and governance to ensure sustainable and responsible shipping practices.

In conclusion, harnessing Greenland's renewable energy potential is crucial for a post-global warming future. It requires a comprehensive approach that includes infrastructure development, adaptation strategies, conservation efforts, and respect for indigenous knowledge. By embracing renewable energy, Greenland can not only mitigate the impacts of climate change but also pave the way for a sustainable and prosperous future. This subchapter appeals to ecologists, politicians, journalists, educators, and the public, providing insights into the future of Greenland after global warming and the opportunities and challenges that lie ahead.

Developing Sustainable Infrastructure to Support Renewable Energy

Introduction

As the world grapples with the consequences of global warming, it is crucial to focus on developing sustainable infrastructure to support renewable energy. This subchapter explores the significance of renewable energy sources in Greenland and the steps taken to build a reliable and resilient infrastructure to harness them. Addressed to ecologists, politicians, journalists, educators, and the public, this chapter aims to highlight the potential of renewable energy and its role in shaping a post-global warming future for Greenland.

Harnessing Renewable Energy Sources

Greenland is blessed with abundant renewable energy sources, including wind, solar, hydro, and geothermal. Exploiting these resources can reduce the dependence on fossil fuels and mitigate the impacts of climate change. By investing in research and development, Greenland can optimize the efficiency of renewable energy technologies and enhance their integration into the energy grid.

Building Sustainable Infrastructure

Developing sustainable infrastructure is crucial for the successful adoption of renewable energy sources. This includes the construction of wind farms, solar power plants, and hydroelectric facilities. Moreover, smart grids and energy storage systems must be implemented to ensure a stable and reliable energy supply. These infrastructure developments require collaboration between policymakers, engineers, and the private sector to guarantee their long-term sustainability and affordability.

Benefits of Renewable Energy Infrastructure

A robust renewable energy infrastructure offers numerous benefits for Greenland. Firstly, it reduces greenhouse gas emissions, thereby combating climate change. Secondly, it enhances energy security by decreasing reliance on imported fossil fuels. Thirdly, it creates job opportunities and stimulates economic growth through the establishment of renewable energy industries. Additionally, renewable energy can provide power to remote communities, improving their quality of life.

Overcoming Challenges

While the development of sustainable infrastructure is vital, it comes with its own set of challenges. The harsh Arctic climate and remote locations pose logistical difficulties during construction and maintenance. However, with innovative engineering solutions and adequate investment, these challenges can be overcome. Collaboration with international partners can also provide valuable expertise and financial support in building a resilient renewable energy infrastructure.

Conclusion

Developing sustainable infrastructure to support renewable energy is a critical step towards a post-global warming future for Greenland. By harnessing its abundant renewable energy sources and building resilient infrastructure, Greenland can reduce its carbon footprint, enhance energy security, create economic opportunities, and protect its unique ecosystems. This requires the collective efforts of ecologists, politicians, journalists, educators, and the public, along with international cooperation and effective governance. Together, we can pave the way for a sustainable and prosperous Greenland in the face of global warming.

Chapter 4: Adaptation and Resilience Strategies for Greenlandic Communities in a Warmer Future

Understanding the Vulnerabilities of Greenlandic Communities

As the impacts of global warming continue to unfold, it is crucial to understand the vulnerabilities faced by Greenlandic communities. This subchapter aims to shed light on the challenges and risks that these communities encounter in a changing climate. By doing so, it provides valuable insights for ecologists, politicians, journalists, educators, and the public, allowing them to comprehend the urgent need for action and support.

Greenland, with its unique cultural heritage and fragile ecosystems, is particularly susceptible to the effects of global warming. Rising temperatures, melting ice, and changing weather patterns pose significant threats to the livelihoods and well-being of the Greenlandic people. The subchapter delves into these vulnerabilities, exploring their impact on various aspects of life in Greenland.

One of the critical areas covered in this subchapter is the adaptation and resilience strategies for Greenlandic communities in a warmer future. It delves into the challenges faced by these communities in adapting to the changing environment, such as the loss of traditional hunting grounds and the need for new livelihood alternatives. It also highlights the importance of indigenous knowledge and traditional practices in helping communities navigate these changes.

Furthermore, the subchapter addresses the impacts of global warming on Greenlandic culture, language, and identity. It examines how the changing environment is affecting traditional practices, such as dog sledding and hunting, which are deeply intertwined with the cultural fabric of Greenland. It also explores the potential loss of language and cultural heritage as a result of these changes and the need to preserve and promote Greenlandic identity in a warmer future.

Notably, the subchapter recognizes the significance of international cooperation and governance for the future of Greenland after global warming. It emphasizes the need for collaborative efforts between nations, policymakers, and communities to mitigate the impacts of climate change and ensure a sustainable future for Greenland.

Overall, this subchapter provides a comprehensive understanding of the vulnerabilities faced by Greenlandic communities. By addressing topics such as adaptation strategies, cultural impacts, and international cooperation, it aims to inspire action and support among ecologists, politicians, journalists, educators, and the public. Only through a collective effort can we navigate the challenges of a post-global warming Greenland and ensure a sustainable future for all.

Building Resilience and Adaptation Strategies for a Changing Climate

In a world where climate change is rapidly altering the face of our planet, Greenland finds itself at the forefront of these changes. As the ice melts and global temperatures rise, Greenland must develop resilience and adaptation strategies to navigate this post-global warming future. This subchapter explores various facets of building resilience and adaptation in Greenland, addressing a wide range of audiences, including ecologists, politicians, journalists, educators, and the public.

One key aspect to consider is the future of Greenland after global warming. With rising temperatures, Greenland's landscape will undergo significant transformations, impacting its ecosystems, biodiversity, and overall sustainability. This section delves into the challenges and opportunities that lie ahead for the country, emphasizing the need for proactive measures to protect and preserve its unique environment.

Another crucial area to explore is sustainable tourism in Greenland post-global warming. As the ice melts, new opportunities arise for tourism, but it is essential to ensure that these activities are conducted in an environmentally responsible manner. This subchapter examines strategies for sustainable tourism development, such as implementing eco-friendly practices and promoting awareness among tourists.

Renewable energy sources and infrastructure development also play a vital role in Greenland's future. As traditional energy sources become increasingly unsustainable, transitioning to renewable energy becomes imperative. This section discusses the potential of renewable energy sources like wind, solar, and hydroelectric power in Greenland, as well as the necessary infrastructure development to support these initiatives.

Adaptation and resilience strategies for Greenlandic communities in a warmer future are paramount. This subchapter explores the challenges faced by communities in adapting to a changing climate, including the loss of traditional livelihoods and the need for new skills and resources. It highlights the importance of community engagement, education, and the empowerment of residents in building resilience.

Conservation and management of Greenland's unique ecosystems and biodiversity are central to ensuring the country's long-term sustainability. This section examines the best practices for managing and protecting Greenland's natural resources, including the establishment of protected areas, sustainable fishing practices, and responsible wildlife management.

The economic opportunities and challenges in post-global warming Greenland are also discussed, recognizing the potential for new industries such as renewable energy, sustainable tourism, and resource extraction. However, it is crucial to balance economic growth with environmental conservation and social responsibility.

The subchapter also explores the impacts of climate change on Greenlandic culture, language, and identity. As traditional ways of life are threatened, it is essential to preserve and promote indigenous knowledge and traditional practices in a changing Greenlandic landscape.

Moreover, the implications of melting ice and potential resource extraction in Greenland's changing environment are examined. This section delves into the challenges and opportunities associated with resource extraction, emphasizing the importance of sustainable practices and responsible governance.

International cooperation and governance are critical for the future of Greenland after global warming. This subchapter highlights the need for collaborative efforts among nations, organizations, and communities to address climate change, protect Greenland's interests, and ensure a sustainable and resilient future.

In conclusion, building resilience and adaptation strategies for a changing climate is vital for Greenland's post-global warming future. By examining various aspects such as sustainable tourism, renewable energy, adaptation strategies, conservation, economic opportunities, indigenous knowledge, and international cooperation, this subchapter provides a comprehensive guide for ecologists, politicians, journalists, educators, and the public interested in navigating the challenges and opportunities that lie ahead for Greenland.

Chapter 5: Conservation and Management of Greenland's Unique Ecosystems and Biodiversity

Preserving Greenland's Fragile Ecosystems and Biodiversity

Introduction:

Greenland, the largest island in the world, is facing significant challenges due to global warming and the rapidly changing climate. As the ice melts and temperatures rise, the delicate ecosystems and biodiversity in Greenland are at risk. Preserving these fragile ecosystems is of utmost importance to ensure the sustainability and resilience of the island in a post-global warming future. This subchapter explores the various strategies and initiatives aimed at conserving Greenland's unique ecosystems and biodiversity.

Conservation Efforts:

Efforts to conserve Greenland's ecosystems and biodiversity should focus on protecting and restoring habitats, promoting sustainable land use practices, and implementing effective wildlife management plans.

This includes establishing protected areas, such as national parks and nature reserves, where vulnerable species can thrive and migrate freely. Collaboration between ecologists, politicians, and local communities is crucial to ensure the success of these conservation efforts.

Sustainable Tourism:

Greenland's tourism industry is expected to grow as the effects of global warming make the island more accessible. However, it is imperative to develop sustainable tourism practices that minimize negative impacts on the environment and contribute to the conservation of ecosystems. Educating tourists about the fragility of Greenland's ecosystems and promoting responsible behavior is essential. Additionally, offering eco-friendly accommodations, transportation, and tour options can help reduce the industry's ecological footprint.

Renewable Energy Sources:

To mitigate the impacts of global warming and reduce dependency on fossil fuels, Greenland should invest in renewable energy sources. This includes harnessing wind, solar, and hydroelectric power to meet the island's energy needs. Developing the necessary infrastructure, such as energy grids and storage systems, will be essential for a successful transition to sustainable energy. This shift towards renewables will not only reduce greenhouse gas emissions but also protect Greenland's ecosystems from further degradation caused by resource extraction.

Indigenous Knowledge and Traditional Practices:

Greenland's indigenous communities have a deep understanding of the land and its ecosystems. Recognizing and integrating indigenous knowledge and traditional practices into conservation efforts can significantly contribute to the preservation of Greenland's biodiversity. By combining scientific research with traditional ecological knowledge, we can gain valuable insights into the island's ecosystems and develop effective conservation strategies that respect indigenous cultures.

International Cooperation and Governance:

Preserving Greenland's fragile ecosystems and biodiversity requires international collaboration and cooperation. Governments, organizations, and stakeholders must work together to establish effective governance structures and policies that prioritize conservation. Sharing knowledge, best practices, and resources will be crucial in navigating the challenges presented by post-global warming Greenland.

Conclusion:

Preserving Greenland's fragile ecosystems and biodiversity is essential for the island's sustainable future. By implementing conservation strategies, promoting sustainable tourism, investing in renewable energy, integrating indigenous knowledge, and fostering international cooperation, we can ensure the resilience and continued existence of Greenland's unique ecosystems and biodiversity. The responsibility lies with ecologists, politicians, journalists, educators, and the public to actively engage in the preservation of Greenland's natural heritage for generations to come.

Sustainable Management Practices for Greenland's Natural Resources

Introduction:

As Greenland faces a post-global warming future, it is crucial to develop sustainable management practices for its natural resources. This subchapter explores the various strategies and initiatives that can ensure the responsible utilization and conservation of Greenland's valuable resources. Targeting ecologists, politicians, journalists, educators, and the general public, this chapter aims to shed light on the importance of sustainable management practices and their potential impacts on the future of Greenland.

Sustainable Resource Exploitation:

Greenland's changing environment presents opportunities for resource extraction, but it is vital to approach this with caution. By implementing sustainable practices, such as responsible mining techniques, waste management, and strict environmental regulations,

Greenland can minimize negative impacts on its ecosystems while maximizing economic benefits. Engaging with indigenous communities and incorporating their traditional knowledge is crucial to strike a balance between resource exploitation and cultural preservation.

Conservation and Biodiversity:

Greenland's unique ecosystems and biodiversity must be protected and conserved. This subchapter highlights the need for establishing protected areas, implementing effective wildlife management plans, and promoting sustainable fishing practices. Collaborative efforts between scientists, policymakers, and local communities can ensure the preservation of Greenland's delicate ecosystems, safeguarding their resilience in the face of a warmer future.

Renewable Energy and Infrastructure:

Transitioning to renewable energy sources is a crucial aspect of sustainable management practices in Greenland. This subchapter explores the potential for wind, solar, and hydropower projects, along with the development of efficient infrastructure. By investing in clean energy technologies, Greenland can reduce its dependence on fossil fuels, mitigate climate change, and create new economic opportunities.

Adaptation and Resilience:

The changing climate poses significant challenges for Greenlandic communities. This subchapter emphasizes the importance of adaptation and resilience strategies, including the construction of climate-resilient infrastructure, early warning systems, and community-based initiatives. By empowering local communities and integrating traditional knowledge, Greenland can enhance its capacity to cope with the impacts of global warming.

Conclusion:

Sustainable management practices for Greenland's natural resources are crucial for the future of the country. By adopting responsible resource exploitation methods, conserving biodiversity, promoting renewable energy, and implementing adaptation strategies, Greenland can navigate the post-global warming era while safeguarding its environment, culture, and economy. International cooperation and effective governance will play a pivotal role in ensuring the successful implementation of sustainable practices and securing a sustainable future for Greenland and its people.

Chapter 6: Economic Opportunities and Challenges in a Post-Global Warming Greenland

Exploring New Economic Opportunities in a Warmer Greenland

As the effects of global warming continue to reshape Greenland, the future of the world's largest island holds both challenges and opportunities. In this subchapter, we delve into the potential economic prospects that a warmer Greenland may offer.

One of the critical areas that could see tremendous growth is sustainable tourism. As the ice melts and unveils new landscapes, tourists from all over the world will be drawn to experience the unique beauty and biodiversity of Greenland. With careful planning and a focus on sustainability, tourism can become a vital source of income for local communities while also fostering a deeper appreciation for the fragile Arctic ecosystem.

Renewable energy sources and infrastructure development will play a crucial role in a post-global warming Greenland. The abundance of sunlight and wind can be harnessed to generate clean energy, reducing reliance on fossil fuels. This transition will require significant investment in infrastructure, creating jobs, and stimulating economic growth. Moreover, exporting renewable energy to nearby regions can further boost Greenland's economy and contribute to global efforts in combating climate change.

Adaptation and resilience strategies for Greenlandic communities are paramount in the face of a warmer future. As traditional livelihoods such as fishing and hunting are affected, alternative economic activities must be explored. For example, the cultivation of new crops and the expansion of aquaculture can provide opportunities for sustainable agriculture and food production. Additionally, the development of innovative industries, such as biotechnology and green manufacturing, can help diversify Greenland's economy and create employment opportunities for the local population.

Conservation and management of Greenland's unique ecosystems and biodiversity will be essential for sustainable economic development. Protecting the pristine landscapes, wildlife, and marine resources will ensure their long-term viability and attractiveness to tourists. Collaborative efforts between government agencies, indigenous communities, and environmental organizations will be crucial in implementing effective conservation strategies.

While resource extraction may become more accessible with melting ice, careful consideration must be given to the environmental impact. Responsible extraction of minerals and other natural resources can contribute to Greenland's economy. Still, it should be done in a manner that minimizes harm to fragile ecosystems and respects the rights of indigenous communities.

International cooperation and governance will play a crucial role in shaping the future of Greenland. Collaboration between governments, scientists, and stakeholders is necessary to address the complex challenges and opportunities that a warmer Greenland presents. By sharing knowledge, expertise, and resources, nations can work together toward a sustainable and prosperous future for Greenland and the planet as a whole.

In conclusion, a warmer Greenland brings forth new economic opportunities, but these must be pursued with a solid commitment to sustainability, conservation, and the well-being of local communities. By embracing innovation, international cooperation, and responsible practices, Greenland can navigate the post-global warming future and thrive in a changing world.

Addressing Challenges and Ensuring Sustainable Economic Growth

In the face of the rapidly changing climate, Greenland is at a critical juncture. As the ice melts and the landscape transforms, it becomes imperative to address the challenges and ensure sustainable economic growth for the future. This subchapter explores the various aspects that need to be considered to navigate a post-global warming future in Greenland.

One of the critical areas of concern is the future of tourism in Greenland. As the ice recedes, new opportunities arise for sustainable tourism. The subchapter delves into the potential for developing responsible tourism practices that minimize environmental impact and contribute to the local economy. It also discusses the importance of preserving Greenland's unique cultural heritage and indigenous knowledge, which can be harnessed to create authentic and immersive experiences for visitors.

Renewable energy sources and infrastructure development play a crucial role in achieving sustainability. The subchapter examines the possibilities of harnessing Greenland's vast renewable energy potential, such as hydroelectric, wind, and solar power. It also explores the challenges and opportunities associated with developing infrastructure to support a green economy, including the establishment of efficient transportation networks and energy grids.

Adaptation and resilience strategies for Greenlandic communities are essential in the face of a warmer future. The subchapter discusses the need for community-based approaches that empower local populations to cope with the changing environment. It highlights the importance of integrating traditional knowledge with scientific advancements to develop effective adaptation measures that protect livelihoods and enhance community resilience.

Conservation and management of Greenland's unique ecosystems and biodiversity are paramount. The subchapter emphasizes the need for comprehensive conservation strategies that safeguard Greenland's natural heritage while allowing for sustainable development. It explores the potential for establishing protected areas, promoting sustainable fishing practices, and mitigating the impacts of resource extraction on delicate ecosystems.

The economic opportunities and challenges in post-global warming Greenland are explored in-depth. The subchapter analyzes the potential for new industries, such as renewable energy, tourism, and resource extraction, while also addressing the need for diversification and sustainable economic practices.

Furthermore, the subchapter acknowledges the profound impacts on Greenlandic culture, language, and identity in a warmer future. It examines the ways in which the changing environment shapes cultural practices and highlights the importance of preserving and revitalizing indigenous traditions in a rapidly evolving landscape.

The implications of melting ice and potential resource extraction are also discussed. The subchapter explores the environmental, social, and economic consequences of resource extraction, emphasizing the need for responsible and sustainable practices that minimize harm to the fragile ecosystem.

International cooperation and governance are crucial for the future of Greenland. The subchapter emphasizes the need for collaboration between governments, organizations, and communities to address the challenges and seize the opportunities presented by a post-global warming Greenland. It explores the potential for international partnerships in areas such as research, technology transfer, and climate change mitigation.

In conclusion, addressing challenges and ensuring sustainable economic growth in post-global warming Greenland requires a comprehensive and multifaceted approach. By considering the future of tourism, renewable energy sources, adaptation strategies, conservation efforts, economic opportunities, cultural preservation, resource extraction, and international cooperation, Greenland can navigate a sustainable and prosperous path forward.

Chapter 7: Indigenous Knowledge and Traditional Practices in a Changing Greenlandic Landscape

The Importance of Indigenous Knowledge and Traditional Practices

In the face of a rapidly changing climate and a warmer future, we must recognize and value the importance of indigenous knowledge and traditional practices in Greenland. This subchapter aims to shed light on the significance of indigenous knowledge and traditional methods in navigating a post-global warming future in Greenland.

Indigenous knowledge, accumulated over centuries by Greenlandic communities, holds a wealth of information about the local environment, natural resources, weather patterns, and sustainable practices. This knowledge is deeply rooted in a close relationship with the land, water, and ice and has been passed down through generations. It offers unique insights and solutions that can help us adapt and thrive in a changing world.

Traditional practices, such as hunting, fishing, and herding, have sustained Greenlandic communities for centuries. They have fostered a deep understanding of the delicate balance between humans and nature, emphasizing sustainable resource management and conservation. These practices have allowed communities to adapt to the harsh Arctic environment and have become intertwined with their cultural identity.

As ecologists, politicians, journalists, educators, and the public, we must recognize and respect the value of indigenous knowledge and traditional practices. By incorporating this knowledge into our decision-making processes, we can develop sustainable strategies for the future of Greenland.

For sustainable tourism in post-global warming Greenland, indigenous knowledge can guide the development of responsible tourism practices that respect local customs and protect fragile ecosystems. It can also enhance visitors' experiences by offering a deeper understanding of the cultural heritage and natural wonders of Greenland.

Similarly, when planning for renewable energy sources and infrastructure development, indigenous knowledge can inform the selection of appropriate technologies and locations that minimize the impact on the environment and respect the rights and needs of local communities.

Adaptation and resilience strategies for Greenlandic communities in a warmer future can benefit from indigenous knowledge by incorporating traditional practices that have sustained communities for generations. This can include plans for preserving food, managing water resources, and building resilient infrastructure.

Conservation and management of Greenland's unique ecosystems and biodiversity can be strengthened by indigenous knowledge, which can provide valuable insights into the behaviors and habitats of local wildlife. This knowledge can inform conservation efforts, including the establishment of protected areas and the sustainable management of fisheries.

In a post-global warming Greenland, economic opportunities and challenges will arise. Indigenous knowledge can guide the exploration and extraction of potential resources by ensuring that these activities are carried out in an environmentally responsible manner, minimizing negative impacts on the ecosystem.

The impacts of global warming go beyond the physical environment; they also affect Greenlandic culture, language, and identity. Indigenous knowledge can help preserve and promote cultural traditions, languages, and ways of life that are deeply connected to the land, fostering a sense of pride and resilience in the face of change.

International cooperation and governance for the future of Greenland after global warming require the inclusion and recognition of indigenous knowledge and traditional practices. By involving local communities in decision-making processes, we can ensure that their voices are heard, and their rights are respected.

In conclusion, indigenous knowledge and traditional practices hold immense value in a changing Greenlandic landscape. By recognizing, respecting, and incorporating this knowledge into our strategies and decision-making processes, we can navigate a post-global warming future in Greenland in a sustainable, inclusive, and culturally sensitive manner.

Integrating Indigenous Knowledge with Modern Adaptation Strategies

In the face of a post-global warming future, Greenland finds itself at a critical juncture, requiring the integration of indigenous knowledge with modern adaptation strategies. This subchapter explores the vital role of indigenous knowledge in navigating the challenges and opportunities that lie ahead for the future of Greenland.

Indigenous communities in Greenland have a deep understanding of the land, its resources, and the delicate balance of ecosystems. Their traditional knowledge has been passed down through generations, providing invaluable insights into sustainable practices and resilience strategies. By integrating this knowledge with modern adaptation strategies, Greenland can forge a path towards a more sustainable and prosperous future.

One key area where indigenous knowledge can play a significant role is in sustainable tourism. Greenland's unique landscapes, rich cultural heritage, and abundant biodiversity make it an attractive destination for tourists. By incorporating indigenous knowledge into tourism planning and development, we can ensure that this industry respects local traditions, minimizes environmental impact, and benefits local communities.

Renewable energy sources and infrastructure development are another crucial aspect of Greenland's future. Indigenous communities have long relied on sustainable energy sources, such as hydropower and wind energy. By harnessing this knowledge and combining it with modern technology, Greenland can become a leader in renewable energy production. This not only reduces reliance on fossil fuels but also creates economic opportunities and jobs for local communities.

Adaptation and resilience strategies for Greenlandic communities in a warmer future are paramount. Indigenous knowledge can provide insights into traditional practices, such as ice hunting, fishing, and agriculture, which have sustained communities for centuries. By integrating these practices with modern adaptation strategies, we can build resilient communities that can withstand the challenges posed by climate change.

Conservation and management of Greenland's unique ecosystems and biodiversity are essential to preserving its natural heritage. Indigenous knowledge offers invaluable insights into sustainable resource management, including hunting, fishing, and land stewardship practices. By incorporating this knowledge into conservation efforts, we can ensure the long-term preservation of Greenland's fragile ecosystems.

The economic opportunities and challenges in a post-global warming Greenland require careful consideration. Indigenous knowledge can inform sustainable economic development, such as small-scale industries, cultural tourism, and traditional handicrafts. By valuing and supporting these economic activities, we can empower local communities and promote a thriving and diverse economy.

As Greenland's environment changes, so too does its culture, language, and identity. Indigenous knowledge provides a unique perspective on the impacts of climate change on these aspects of Greenlandic society. By acknowledging and supporting indigenous cultural practices and language preservation efforts, we can ensure the continuity of Greenland's rich cultural heritage.

International cooperation and governance will be crucial for the future of Greenland. Indigenous knowledge can contribute to discussions on Arctic shipping routes, trade implications, and resource extraction in a changing environment. By involving indigenous communities in decision-making processes, we can ensure that their voices are heard, and their rights are respected.

In conclusion, integrating indigenous knowledge with modern adaptation strategies is essential for the future of Greenland. By valuing and incorporating traditional practices, sustainable tourism, renewable energy, resilience strategies, conservation efforts, economic opportunities, cultural preservation, and international cooperation, we can navigate a post-global warming future that respects and honors Greenland's unique heritage and ensures a sustainable and prosperous future for all.

Chapter 8: Arctic Shipping Routes and Trade Implications for Greenland After Global Warming

Navigating the Changing Arctic Shipping Routes

As the effects of global warming continue to reshape the Arctic landscape, there has been a significant increase in attention to the potential opening of new shipping routes in the region. This subchapter aims to explore the implications of these changing Arctic shipping routes for Greenland and its future.

For ecologists, it offers an opportunity to study the environmental impact of increased shipping activity in the Arctic. The melting ice has already led to the emergence of new routes, such as the Northern Sea Route and the Northwest Passage, which have the potential to reduce travel distances and shipping times significantly. However, the increased traffic also raises concerns about the potential for accidents and spills, as well as the disturbance of fragile ecosystems and wildlife habitats.

Politicians and journalists need to be aware of the geopolitical implications of these changing routes. With the opening of new shipping lanes, there may be a shift in global trade patterns, leading to economic opportunities for Greenland. However, it also raises questions about the governance of these routes and the involvement of international actors in the region. Cooperation between nations will be crucial to ensure the sustainable and responsible development of Arctic shipping.

Educators can use this subchapter to inform students about the challenges and opportunities presented by the changing Arctic shipping routes. They can explore the economic benefits and potential risks associated with increased shipping activity, as well as the environmental considerations that need to be taken into account.

The public, including tourists, will be interested in understanding how the changing Arctic shipping routes might impact Greenland's economy and infrastructure. Sustainable tourism in Greenland after global warming could benefit from increased accessibility, but it must be managed carefully to avoid negative impacts on the environment and local communities.

In conclusion, the emergence of new Arctic shipping routes presents both opportunities and challenges for Greenland. It is vital that all stakeholders, including ecologists, politicians, journalists, educators, and the public, are well-informed about the implications of these changes. By navigating these routes responsibly and sustainably, Greenland can harness the economic benefits while protecting its unique ecosystems and cultural heritage. International cooperation and governance will be essential in shaping the future of Arctic shipping and ensuring a post-global warming Greenland thrives.

Economic and Trade Opportunities for Greenland in a Thawing Arctic

As the impacts of global warming continue to reshape the Arctic landscape, Greenland finds itself at the center of new economic and trade opportunities. This subchapter delves into the various avenues through which Greenland can harness these opportunities and navigate a post-global warming future.

Renewable energy sources and infrastructure development in Greenland offer promising prospects for economic growth. With the melting ice opening up new areas for exploration, the country can tap into its vast potential for hydroelectric, wind, and solar energy. Investing in renewable energy not only positions Greenland as a leader in sustainable development but also creates employment opportunities and attracts investments from international partners.

Additionally, the thawing Arctic presents a unique chance to develop sustainable tourism in Greenland. The pristine landscapes, unique biodiversity, and cultural heritage of Greenland make it a beautiful destination for ecotourism enthusiasts. By carefully managing the influx of tourists and implementing sustainable practices, Greenland can create a thriving tourism industry that bolsters the local economy while preserving its natural and cultural treasures.

The melting ice also holds the key to potential resource extraction in Greenland's changing environment. With the opening of new shipping routes and the uncovering of previously inaccessible areas, the country can explore the extraction of valuable minerals, oil, and gas reserves. However, it is crucial to balance economic gains with environmental stewardship and ensure that resource extraction is carried out responsibly, taking into consideration the impacts on ecosystems and biodiversity.

Furthermore, international cooperation and governance will play a pivotal role in shaping the future of Greenland. As the Arctic becomes increasingly important in global trade and geopolitics, Greenland needs to engage with international partners, policymakers, and organizations to negotiate fair trade agreements, establish sustainable practices, and protect the rights and interests of indigenous communities.

In conclusion, a thawing Arctic presents both challenges and opportunities for Greenland. By embracing sustainable tourism, renewable energy development, responsible resource extraction, and fostering international cooperation, Greenland can navigate a post-global warming future and build a resilient and prosperous economy. However, it is crucial to prioritize environmental conservation, protect indigenous knowledge and cultural heritage, and ensure the well-being of Greenlandic communities throughout this transformative process. Only through careful planning and collaboration can Greenland seize the economic and trade opportunities that lie ahead while safeguarding its unique ecosystems, biodiversity, and identity.

Chapter 9: Melting Ice and Potential Resource Extraction in Greenland's Changing Environment

Resource Extraction Potential in a Warmer Greenland

Introduction:

As global warming accelerates, Greenland finds itself at the center of attention due to its vast potential for resource extraction. This subchapter explores the opportunities and challenges associated with the changing environment in Greenland and the implications for resource extraction in a warmer future. It delves into the economic, environmental, and social aspects of this issue, addressing the interests of ecologists, politicians, journalists, educators, and the general public.

Exploring Resource Potential:

Greenland's melting ice and thawing permafrost are revealing previously untapped reserves of minerals, oil, and gas. The region is rich in rare earth elements, uranium, gold, and oil, attracting the attention of mining and energy companies worldwide. The opening up of new areas for exploration presents immense economic opportunities for Greenland as it transitions towards a post-global warming future.

Environmental Considerations:

Resource extraction in a warmer Greenland must be approached with caution to minimize adverse environmental impacts. Strict regulations and sustainable practices should be implemented to ensure that extraction activities do not harm delicate ecosystems and biodiversity. Collaboration between scientists, ecologists, and policymakers is crucial to strike a balance between economic development and environmental conservation.

Social and Cultural Impacts:

Resource extraction in Greenland's changing environment has significant implications for local communities and indigenous populations. It is essential to incorporate the perspectives and traditional knowledge of these communities in decision-making processes to safeguard their cultural identity and ensure fair benefit sharing. Education and awareness programs can help promote sustainable practices and long-term community resilience.

International Cooperation and Governance:

Given the global interest in Greenland's resources, international cooperation and governance frameworks are necessary to address resource extraction challenges effectively. Collaborative efforts among governments, NGOs, and industry stakeholders can ensure responsible resource management, minimize conflicts, and maximize economic benefits for Greenland and the international community.

Conclusion:

Resource extraction potential in a warmer Greenland presents a complex set of opportunities and challenges. Balancing economic development with environmental conservation, preserving cultural heritage, and ensuring the well-being of local communities requires careful planning and cooperation. By adopting sustainable practices, incorporating indigenous knowledge, and fostering international collaboration, Greenland can navigate the post-global warming future while harnessing its resource extraction potential responsibly. Ecologists, politicians, journalists, educators, and the general public all play a vital role in shaping this future and must work together to achieve a sustainable and prosperous Greenland.

Balancing Environmental Concerns with Resource Development

In the face of a post-global warming future, Greenland finds itself at a critical crossroads where the delicate balance between environmental concerns and resource development must be carefully navigated. This subchapter explores the complexities and challenges associated with finding a sustainable path forward for the nation, addressing the concerns of ecologists, politicians, journalists, educators, and the general public.

As Greenland's landscape transforms, the future of the nation hinges on the responsible management of its resources. Sustainable tourism emerges as a potential driver for economic growth, offering an opportunity to showcase Greenland's unique natural beauty and cultural heritage. However, it is crucial to strike a balance between attracting visitors and preserving the fragile ecosystems that draw them in the first place.

Additionally, renewable energy sources and infrastructure development play a vital role in reducing Greenland's carbon footprint and achieving sustainability goals. The subchapter delves into the challenges and opportunities associated with harnessing Greenland's vast potential for clean energy, highlighting the need for careful planning and investment in infrastructure.

In the face of a warmer future, adaptation and resilience strategies for Greenlandic communities become paramount. The subchapter explores innovative approaches to mitigate the impacts of climate change on local communities, focusing on the preservation of traditional practices and indigenous knowledge that have sustained Greenlandic culture for centuries.

Conservation and management of Greenland's unique ecosystems and biodiversity also feature prominently in this subchapter. Efforts to protect and restore these ecosystems must be balanced with the potential for responsible resource extraction. The chapter delves into the complexities of managing these competing interests, emphasizing the need for a collaborative approach that brings together scientists, policymakers, and local communities.

The economic opportunities and challenges that arise in a post-global warming Greenland are also examined. As new industries emerge, careful consideration must be given to ensure that economic growth is sustainable inclusive, and respects local values and traditions.

Moreover, the subchapter highlights the impacts of a changing environment on Greenlandic culture, language, and identity. It explores the need to empower indigenous communities to navigate these changes while preserving their cultural heritage.

As Arctic shipping routes open up, trade implications for Greenland are significant. The subchapter explores the potential benefits and risks associated with increased shipping activity, emphasizing the need for international cooperation and governance to ensure sustainable and responsible practices.

Finally, the subchapter delves into the implications of melting ice and potential resource extraction in Greenland's changing environment. It provides an overview of the environmental risks and regulatory challenges associated with resource extraction, underscoring the importance of striking a balance between economic development and environmental protection.

In conclusion, the subchapter "Balancing Environmental Concerns with Resource Development" addresses the multifaceted challenges and opportunities that Greenland faces in a post-global warming future. It calls for a collaborative and inclusive approach that involves ecologists, politicians, journalists, educators, and the general public to ensure a sustainable and prosperous future for Greenland.

Chapter 10: Impacts on Greenlandic Culture, Language, and Identity in a Warmer Future

Cultural Shifts and Challenges in a Changing Greenland

As Greenland's landscape continues to transform in the face of global warming, the implications for its culture, language, and identity are profound. This subchapter explores the cultural shifts and challenges that Greenland is experiencing in its journey towards a post-global warming future.

The melting ice and changing environment in Greenland have direct implications for the indigenous communities that have thrived in this harsh Arctic region for centuries. The Inuit people, who have a deep connection to the land and sea, are now faced with the need to adapt their traditional practices and knowledge to a rapidly changing landscape. This presents both opportunities and challenges as they strive to maintain their cultural heritage while embracing new ways of life.

One of the key challenges lies in preserving Greenland's unique ecosystems and biodiversity. As the ice melts and new species migrate into the region, there is a need for conservation and management strategies to protect these fragile ecosystems. This requires collaboration between scientists, policymakers, and local communities to ensure sustainable practices are implemented.

The economic opportunities and challenges in a post-global warming Greenland are also significant. With the opening of new shipping routes and potential resource extraction, there is potential for economic growth. However, careful planning and sustainable practices are essential to avoid exploitation and ensure the benefits are shared equitably among all stakeholders. This requires international cooperation and governance to regulate these activities and protect the interests of the Greenlandic people.

The impacts on Greenlandic culture, language, and identity are profound. As the environment changes, traditional ways of life are being disrupted, and the younger generation is growing up in a vastly different landscape. Preserving the Greenlandic language, which is deeply tied to the land and cultural identity, becomes crucial in ensuring the survival of the Greenlandic people's heritage.

Education and awareness play a vital role in navigating these cultural shifts and challenges. Educators and journalists have the responsibility to inform the public about the realities of a changing Greenland and the importance of preserving its cultural heritage. Additionally, politicians need to develop adaptation and resilience strategies that prioritize the needs and aspirations of the Greenlandic communities.

In conclusion, the cultural shifts and challenges in a changing Greenland are complex and multifaceted. As ecologists, politicians, journalists, educators, and the public, we must work together to address these challenges and ensure the sustainable future of Greenland's unique culture, language, and identity. International cooperation and governance will play a crucial role in shaping the future of Greenland post-global warming.

Safeguarding Greenlandic Culture and Identity in the Face of Climate Change

Introduction:

As Greenland faces the challenges posed by climate change, it is crucial to address the potential impact on the culture and identity of its people. This subchapter explores the ways in which Greenlandic culture and identity can be safeguarded in the face of a changing climate. The preservation of cultural heritage, language, and traditional practices is vital for the well-being and resilience of Greenlandic communities.

Preserving Cultural Heritage:

Greenland's unique cultural heritage must be protected and celebrated. Efforts should be made to document and preserve traditional practices, such as hunting, fishing, and handicrafts, which play a significant role in the identity of the Greenlandic people. This can be achieved through community-led initiatives, educational programs, and the establishment of cultural centers that showcase and transmit traditional knowledge to future generations.

Language Revitalization:

The Greenlandic language is a cornerstone of the country's cultural identity. In the face of climate change, increased efforts should be made to promote and preserve the language. Language immersion programs, community language schools, and the integration of the language into formal education systems can help revitalize and maintain Greenlandic as a vibrant living language.

Supporting Indigenous Knowledge:

Indigenous knowledge holds invaluable insights into adapting to environmental changes. It is necessary to recognize, respect, and integrate traditional knowledge systems into climate change adaptation strategies. Collaborative research projects between scientists and indigenous communities can ensure that local knowledge is considered and incorporated into decision-making processes.

Cultural Tourism:

Sustainable tourism can provide economic opportunities while also promoting cultural exchange and understanding. By developing tourism initiatives that respect and protect Greenlandic culture, visitors can engage with local communities and traditions, fostering cross-cultural connections and supporting the preservation of cultural identity.

Community Resilience:

Adaptation and resilience strategies should prioritize community engagement and empowerment. Local communities must be involved in decision-making processes to ensure that their needs and concerns are addressed. Supporting community-led initiatives, such as sustainable agriculture, renewable energy projects, and infrastructure development, can foster self-reliance and enhance the resilience of Greenlandic communities.

Conclusion:

Safeguarding Greenlandic culture and identity in the face of climate change is an urgent and complex task. It requires a multifaceted approach that involves preserving cultural heritage, revitalizing the Greenlandic language, supporting indigenous knowledge, promoting sustainable tourism, and empowering local communities. By valuing and protecting the unique cultural identity of Greenland, we can navigate a future that is both resilient and true to its roots. International cooperation and governance play a crucial role in ensuring the preservation of Greenland's culture and identity in the post-global warming era. It is the responsibility of ecologists, politicians, journalists, educators, and the public to take action and safeguard Greenlandic culture for future generations.

Chapter 11: International Cooperation and Governance for the Future of Greenland After Global Warming

Importance of International Cooperation in Addressing Climate Change

In the face of the unprecedented challenges posed by climate change, the importance of international cooperation cannot be overstated. As we navigate the future of Greenland in a post-global warming era, ecologists, politicians, journalists, educators, and the public must understand and actively participate in collaborative efforts to address this global crisis.

Climate change knows no boundaries, and its impacts are felt far beyond national borders. It is a collective problem that requires collaborative solutions. International cooperation is essential to effectively mitigate the causes of climate change and adapt to its consequences.

One key aspect of international cooperation is the sharing of knowledge and best practices. By exchanging information and experiences, scientists, policymakers, and educators can develop a deeper understanding of the complex dynamics of climate change and identify effective strategies for mitigation and adaptation. This knowledge exchange can also facilitate the development and implementation of sustainable tourism practices in Greenland, ensuring that this vital industry thrives while minimizing its ecological footprint.

Renewable energy sources and infrastructure development are crucial components of a sustainable future for Greenland. International cooperation can provide the necessary resources, expertise, and funding to accelerate the transition to renewable energy and develop a resilient infrastructure that can withstand the challenges of a changing climate. Collaboration in these areas can help Greenland become a model for sustainable development, showcasing the potential of renewable energy and green infrastructure.

Adaptation and resilience strategies are paramount for communities in Greenland to thrive in a warmer future. International cooperation can support the development and implementation of these strategies, ensuring that the unique needs and vulnerabilities of Greenlandic communities are addressed. By sharing experiences and resources, we can enhance the resilience of communities and protect their cultural heritage in the face of climate change.

Conservation and management of Greenland's unique ecosystems and biodiversity require international collaboration. By working together, we can establish protected areas, implement sustainable management practices, and conserve the fragile ecosystems that make Greenland so unique. This cooperation can also facilitate scientific research and monitoring efforts, leading to a better understanding of the impacts of climate change on these ecosystems.

Economic opportunities and challenges in post-global warming Greenland need to be approached with a global perspective. International cooperation can help diversify the economy, foster innovation, and create new sustainable industries while also addressing potential challenges such as resource extraction and trade implications. By working together, we can ensure that economic development is balanced with environmental stewardship and social equity.

Lastly, international cooperation and governance are crucial for the future of Greenland after global warming. Collaboration between nations, organizations, and stakeholders can lead to the development of effective policies, agreements, and frameworks to address climate change on a global scale. By fostering dialogue, cooperation, and shared responsibility, we can collectively shape a sustainable and resilient future for Greenland and the planet.

In conclusion, international cooperation is of paramount importance in addressing climate change and shaping the future of Greenland. By working together, we can develop effective strategies, share knowledge and resources, and create a sustainable and resilient future for all. It is our collective responsibility to act now and ensure a brighter future for generations to come.

Governance Frameworks for Sustainable Development in Greenland

As Greenland faces the challenges of a post-global warming future, the need for effective governance frameworks to ensure sustainable development becomes paramount. This subchapter explores the crucial role of governance in navigating the path toward a resilient and prosperous Greenland. It addresses the concerns of ecologists, politicians, journalists, educators, and the public, shedding light on the diverse aspects of sustainable development in the region.

Greenland's future hinges on the effective management of its resources and the preservation of its unique ecosystems and biodiversity. A comprehensive governance framework must prioritize conservation efforts and establish robust management systems to protect these invaluable assets. Collaborative partnerships between government agencies, indigenous communities, and environmental organizations will be crucial in achieving this goal.

Another critical aspect of sustainable development in Greenland is the promotion of renewable energy sources and infrastructure development. By harnessing its vast potential for wind, solar, and hydroelectric power, Greenland can reduce its reliance on fossil fuels and transition towards a greener future. Robust governance frameworks should encourage investment in renewable energy projects, ensuring the development of sustainable infrastructure that supports economic growth while minimizing environmental impact.

In a warmer future, Greenlandic communities will face unique challenges and require adaptation and resilience strategies. Effective governance frameworks should prioritize the empowerment of these communities, ensuring their active participation in decision-making processes and providing access to resources and support for adaptation measures. By integrating indigenous knowledge and traditional practices into governance strategies, Greenland can capitalize on the wisdom of its people and foster a more sustainable and culturally rich future.

Furthermore, the changing climate will open new opportunities for economic growth in Greenland, including sustainable tourism and potential resource extraction. Governance frameworks must strike a delicate balance between economic development and environmental protection, ensuring that these opportunities are harnessed responsibly and sustainably. International cooperation will be crucial in establishing guidelines and regulations to govern these activities and mitigate potential negative impacts.

In conclusion, effective governance frameworks are essential for steering Greenland towards a sustainable and prosperous future. By prioritizing conservation, renewable energy, adaptation, and resilience and fostering collaboration between various stakeholders, Greenland can navigate the challenges of a post-global warming era. The preservation of its unique ecosystems, cultural heritage, and economic opportunities will depend on the implementation of robust governance frameworks that prioritize sustainability and resilience. Only through international cooperation and inclusive decision-making processes can Greenland secure a prosperous future for generations to come.

Conclusion: Navigating a Post-Global Warming Future for Greenland

Summary of Key Findings and Recommendations for Action

In the book "Greenland 2050: Navigating a Post-Global Warming Future," we have explored various aspects of Greenland's future after global warming. This subchapter aims to provide a summary of the essential findings and recommendations for action. Addressed to ecologists, politicians, journalists, educators, and the public, this section covers a wide range of niches to ensure a holistic understanding of the challenges and opportunities that lie ahead.

One of the crucial areas discussed is the future of Greenland after global warming. The book highlights the need for comprehensive strategies that focus on sustainable tourism, renewable energy sources, infrastructure development, and adaptation and resilience measures for

Greenlandic communities. It emphasizes the importance of conservation and management of Greenland's unique ecosystems and biodiversity, as well as the economic opportunities and challenges that arise in a post-global warming Greenland.

Furthermore, the book recognizes the significance of indigenous knowledge and traditional practices in navigating a changing Greenlandic landscape. It stresses the importance of preserving and integrating this knowledge into future decision-making processes.

Another critical aspect explored is the impact of melting ice and potential resource extraction in Greenland's changing environment. The book emphasizes the need for responsible resource extraction practices to minimize ecological damage and protect the fragile Arctic ecosystem.

The cultural and social implications of a warmer future for Greenland are also examined. The book emphasizes the importance of safeguarding Greenlandic culture, language, and identity in the face of changing climatic conditions. It encourages initiatives that promote cultural preservation and adaptation.

Lastly, the book highlights the need for international cooperation and governance to address the challenges faced by Greenland. It underscores the importance of collaborative efforts in developing sustainable policies, sharing knowledge, and mobilizing resources.

Based on these key findings, the book presents recommendations for action. It calls for the formulation and implementation of policies that prioritize sustainable tourism, investment in renewable energy infrastructure, and the development of adaptation and resilience strategies for Greenlandic communities. The book also recommends the establishment of protected areas to conserve Greenland's unique ecosystems and biodiversity.

Moreover, it suggests the promotion of economic diversification and the creation of opportunities in sectors such as sustainable agriculture, fisheries, and clean technology. The book also stresses the importance of integrating indigenous knowledge into decision-making processes and fostering cultural preservation initiatives.

Lastly, the book advocates for international cooperation and the establishment of effective governance structures to address the challenges faced by Greenland in a post-global warming future. It emphasizes the need for collaboration on issues related to Arctic shipping routes, resource extraction, and climate change mitigation and adaptation.

In conclusion, the subchapter "Summary of Key Findings and Recommendations for Action" highlights the need for comprehensive strategies and collaborative efforts to navigate a post-global warming future in Greenland. By implementing these recommendations, we can ensure a sustainable and resilient future for Greenland and its communities.

Special Chapter: Benefits to Greenland of a Warmer Climate

While climate change brings a host of challenges and adverse impacts globally, a warming climate has some potential benefits for Greenland specifically. However, it's essential to approach this topic with caution, as the consequences of climate change are multifaceted and can vary over time. Here are some perceived benefits of a warmer climate for Greenland:

1. **Improved Agriculture**: As temperatures rise, the growing season in Greenland becomes longer, and the range of crops that can be cultivated expands. Areas that were once too cold for farming may become arable, which could help increase local food production.

2. **Increased Access to Minerals**: Melting ice is revealing a wealth of minerals, including rare earth elements, iron, zinc, gold, and diamonds. These resources could potentially be exploited, bringing economic benefits to Greenland.

3. **Oil and Gas Exploration**: The melting of Arctic ice can make it easier to access potential oil and gas reserves. While this has geopolitical, environmental, and economic implications, there's potential for economic development for Greenland if reserves are found and can be responsibly exploited.

4. **Expanded Fishing Industry**: Changes in sea temperatures can lead to shifts in fish populations. Some fish species might move northward into Greenlandic waters, potentially enhancing the local fishing industry.

5. **Tourism**: With less ice and milder temperatures, Greenland might become a more attractive destination for tourists. The longer summer season could draw visitors for hiking, fishing, and witnessing the unique Arctic landscapes.

6. **New Shipping Routes**: The melting of Arctic ice is opening up new shipping routes. The Northwest Passage and Northern Sea Route could become more navigable, offering shorter transit times between Asia, Europe, and North America. While Greenland is not directly on these routes, its proximity could allow it to serve as a logistical or service hub.

7. **Infrastructure Development**: In some areas, a milder climate might make it easier to develop infrastructure without the constraints of extreme cold for prolonged periods.

8. **Biodiversity Changes**: While the loss of some species adapted to colder climates is a concern, a warmer Greenland might also see the introduction of new species, leading to a shift in biodiversity.

However, it's vital to remember that the benefits come with significant challenges. Melting ice contributes to global sea level rise, which can have devastating effects elsewhere in the world. Moreover, rapid changes in the environment can disrupt traditional ways of life for the indigenous populations of Greenland. The potential for resource extraction brings with it environmental risks and the challenge of ensuring sustainable and equitable development. Thus, while there are potential benefits, they need to be weighed against these broader concerns.

Improved agriculture

Certainly, Greenland's agriculture in the context of a warming climate is a particularly fascinating area of study. As the global climate warms, and specifically as temperatures rise in traditionally colder regions such as Greenland, the agricultural landscape is undergoing changes:

1. **Extended Growing Season**: One of the most immediate benefits of a warmer climate for any agricultural setting is the extension of the growing season. In Greenland, this could

mean that crops have a longer period to mature, potentially leading to larger yields.

2. **Diversity of Crops**: Historically, the cold climate of Greenland limited the variety of crops that farmers could grow. With the temperatures rising, it's possible to cultivate a broader range of crops. Vegetables such as potatoes, turnips, and carrots are becoming more common, and there's potential for even more variety in the future.

3. **Increased Local Food Production**: Greater agricultural output could reduce Greenland's dependence on imported food. This is significant because imported food in Greenland is costly due to its remote location. By producing more locally, Greenland could achieve a degree of food self-sufficiency, leading to economic savings and increased food security.

4. **New Agricultural Opportunities**: Warmer temperatures and melting glaciers are turning some areas into potential farmlands. As more land becomes arable, there's an opportunity for agriculture to expand in Greenland.

5. **Livestock Farming**: Alongside crop farming, there's potential for expanded livestock farming. The warmer climate allows for better grazing opportunities for sheep and even the possibility of introducing new types of livestock that were previously unsuitable for Greenland's climate.

6. **Economic Growth**: If managed sustainably, increased agricultural output could contribute to Greenland's economy. This is especially relevant as Greenland seeks to diversify its economy, which is currently heavily dependent on fishing and subsidies from Denmark.

7. **Cultural and Social Impacts**: Renewed interest in agriculture could lead to a reconnection with the land and farming traditions. It might also bring about shifts in societal structures, lifestyles, and even diets.

However, there are challenges and considerations:

- **Soil Quality**: While the ice melt might expose more land, the soil quality is not always ideal for agriculture. It might require efforts to enrich and manage the soil to make it conducive to farming.
- **Pest and Diseases**: New pests and diseases, previously not native or common in Greenland, might become a challenge for local agriculture with the warming temperatures.
- **Sustainability**: Rapid expansion of agriculture could have environmental implications. Ensuring that growth is sustainable and does not harm local ecosystems is crucial.
- **Water Management**: While melting glaciers provide freshwater, managing this resource efficiently, especially in light of potential future reductions as glaciers recede, is essential.
- **Traditional Livelihoods**: Rapid shifts in the economy and livelihoods might impact traditional ways of life, and there's a need to balance growth with preserving cultural traditions.

In conclusion, while a warming climate presents opportunities for improved agriculture in Greenland, careful and sustainable management is crucial to ensure long-term benefits.

Increased access to minerals

As Greenland's ice sheet retreats due to a warming climate, vast tracts of land previously covered by ice are being exposed, revealing a wealth of mineral resources. This potential mineral boom can have significant implications for Greenland's economy, geopolitics, and environment. Here are some aspects of this increased access:

1. **Diverse Mineral Deposits**: Greenland is believed to possess an array of mineral resources including:
    - **Rare Earth Elements (REEs)**: Greenland's potential

reserves of REEs, used in various high-tech applications like smartphones, renewable energy technologies, and defense systems, are particularly significant. The Kvanefjeld project in southern Greenland, for instance, is one of the largest untapped REE sites globally.

- **Precious and Base Metals**: There are indications of significant deposits of gold, platinum, palladium, nickel, copper, and zinc.
- **Uranium**: Alongside REEs, there's potential for significant uranium deposits, which can be used for nuclear energy.
- **Iron Ore**: Deposits have been identified in various regions.
- **Gemstones**: Particularly, rubies and sapphires have been found in Greenland.

2. **Economic Implications**: If exploited, these mineral resources can provide a significant boost to Greenland's economy, which historically has been reliant on fishing, tourism, and grants from Denmark. Revenue from mining can potentially pave the way for economic independence.

3. **Geopolitical Significance**: Given the global demand for many of these minerals, especially REEs, Greenland's reserves can have geopolitical implications. The increasing interest of major powers, including China, the US, and EU nations, in Greenland's mineral potential reflects this geopolitical dimension.

4. **Infrastructure Development**: The exploitation of these minerals might lead to enhanced infrastructure in Greenland, including roads, ports, and facilities related to mining activities. This development can aid in further opening up the region for other economic activities.

5. **Job Creation**: Mining projects can generate employment opportunities, leading to socio-economic benefits for the local population.

6. **Environmental Concerns**: Mining, especially open-pit mining, can have significant environmental consequences. This includes habitat disruption, water pollution, and potential risks associated with radioactive materials if uranium is mined. Given Greenland's fragile Arctic ecosystem, sustainable practices are essential.

7. **Cultural and Social Impacts**: There's a need to ensure that the rights and interests of the indigenous Inuit population are protected. Mining projects can lead to shifts in traditional lifestyles, and not always positively. Ensuring local communities have a say in decisions and benefit from mining is crucial.

8. **Regulatory Framework**: As Greenland opens up to more mining, there will be a need for robust regulatory frameworks to ensure responsible extraction, taking into account environmental protections, safety standards, and equitable distribution of benefits.

9. **Volatile Commodity Prices**: Dependence on minerals can expose Greenland's economy to the volatility of global commodity prices. A sustainable, diversified economic approach would be necessary to guard against potential downturns in mineral prices.

In summary, while the melting of Greenland's ice sheet presents significant mineral opportunities, it's crucial to approach exploitation responsibly. Balancing the immediate economic gains with long-term environmental, cultural, and socio-economic considerations will determine the overall benefit to Greenland and its people.

Oil and gas exploration

The prospects for oil and gas exploration in Greenland, especially in offshore regions, have been eyed with interest by energy companies and geopolitical analysts alike. As climate change leads to the melting of Arctic ice, new areas become more accessible for exploration and potential exploitation. Here are some details and considerations related to Greenland's oil and gas prospects in the context of a warming climate:

1. **Potential Reserves**: Geological surveys indicate that there might be significant oil and gas reserves offshore Greenland, especially in the northeastern and northwestern parts. The U.S. Geological Survey (USGS) has estimated that the Arctic holds about 13% of the world's undiscovered oil and 30% of its undiscovered natural gas, with Greenland's waters potentially housing a significant portion of these reserves.

2. **Easier Access**: The retreating ice in the Arctic is making certain areas more navigable, thus potentially easing the logistics of exploration. However, even with melting ice, the Arctic environment remains challenging, and exploration activities are limited to specific months of the year when conditions are more favorable.

3. **Economic Boost**: If commercially viable reserves are found and exploited, Greenland stands to benefit substantially from the revenues. Such an economic boost could play a role in its aspirations for greater autonomy from Denmark or even full independence.

4. **Geopolitical Interest**: Given the global demand for energy, the Arctic, and by extension, Greenland, is becoming a region of heightened geopolitical interest. Major powers, including the USA, Russia, China, and EU nations, are keenly watching developments in the region.

5. **Environmental Concerns**: Oil and gas exploration and extraction, especially in such a fragile environment as the

Arctic, come with significant environmental risks. An oil spill in Arctic waters would have catastrophic ecological consequences and be challenging to contain due to the region's remoteness and harsh conditions.

6. **Technological Challenges**: The Arctic environment poses specific challenges that require advanced technology and significant investments. For example, drilling equipment needs to withstand extreme cold, and infrastructure needs to account for shifting ice.

7. **Indigenous Rights and Concerns**: The indigenous Inuit population of Greenland has expressed concerns about potential environmental degradation and the impact on their traditional way of life. Ensuring that local communities are consulted, their rights are protected, and they benefit from any exploration is essential.

8. **Market Dynamics**: The viability of extracting oil and gas depends on global market prices. With the global push towards renewable energy and the subsequent potential decrease in oil and gas demand, the long-term profitability and feasibility of Arctic oil and gas projects might be challenged.

9. **Regulatory Environment**: Greenland, with the support of Denmark, has been developing its regulatory environment for oil and gas exploration. This includes establishing licensing rounds for exploration blocks, safety protocols, and environmental protections.

10. **Infrastructure Development**: Successful exploration would necessitate the development of infrastructure, from drilling platforms to transportation facilities. This would be a significant undertaking given Greenland's remote and challenging environment.

In conclusion, while a warmer climate might make oil and gas exploration more feasible in Greenland, there are substantial challenges and considerations to weigh. The potential environmental risks and changing global energy dynamics will play pivotal roles in determining the future of Greenland's oil and gas sector.

Fishing industry

The effects of climate change on the marine environment, particularly in the Arctic, are profound. As temperatures rise, shifts in marine ecosystems are impacting the fishing industry, with Greenland positioned at the center of these changes. Here's how a warmer climate might influence Greenland's fishing industry:

1. **Shift in Fish Populations**: As ocean temperatures rise, several fish species are moving northwards to cooler waters. For Greenland, this means the potential influx of commercially valuable fish species that were previously more common in the waters further south. Cod, herring, and mackerel are some of the species that have shown increased presence in Greenlandic waters.

2. **Increased Fish Stocks**: With the northward migration of fish, Greenlandic fishermen might experience increased catches, enhancing the productivity and profitability of the fishing sector, which is already a primary economic driver for Greenland.

3. **Diversification**: Historically, Greenland's fishing industry was primarily focused on shrimp and Greenland halibut. The influx of new fish species offers a chance for diversification, reducing economic dependence on just a couple of species.

4. **Export Opportunities**: With the potential for increased catches and a broader range of species, Greenland could expand its export portfolio, tapping into lucrative global seafood markets. This would be especially significant given the

rising global demand for fish and seafood.

5. **Local Consumption**: An expanded local fishing industry could lead to increased local consumption of a variety of fish species, potentially impacting local diets and food security in a positive manner.

6. **Fisheries Management**: The potential for increased fishing activity underscores the importance of effective fisheries management. Overfishing could pose a threat to fish populations and disrupt the balance of marine ecosystems. Greenland, potentially in collaboration with neighboring countries, will need to implement and enforce sustainable fishing quotas and practices.

7. **Infrastructure and Development**: An expanding fishing industry might necessitate the development of related infrastructure. This includes port facilities, processing plants, storage, and transportation, which can lead to job creation and economic growth.

8. **Environmental Impacts**: While there might be economic benefits, there are environmental concerns as well. The broader impacts of a warming ocean – such as ocean acidification and changes in marine food webs – can affect fish health and populations. Moreover, increased fishing activity can have its own set of environmental consequences if not managed sustainably.

9. **Cultural and Social Impacts**: Fishing is deeply ingrained in Greenlandic culture. Changes in the industry, both positive and negative, can have implications for local communities, traditional practices, and the socio-economic fabric of Greenland.

10. **Geopolitical Considerations**: Fishing rights and territorial waters can become points of contention between countries. As fish populations shift due to changing temperatures, there's

potential for disputes over fishing zones between Greenland and its neighbors.

In summary, while a warmer climate offers opportunities for Greenland's fishing industry, it also presents challenges. Balancing economic growth with sustainable practices and environmental considerations will be crucial for the long-term prosperity and health of both the industry and the marine ecosystems.

Tourism

Climate change and the resulting warmer temperatures are significantly influencing the tourism industry in Greenland. As the Arctic environment undergoes transformation, Greenland presents both new attractions and challenges for tourists and the tourism industry. Here's an overview of how a warmer climate might enhance tourism in Greenland:

1. **Extended Tourist Season**: Traditionally, Greenland's tourism season was relatively short due to its long, cold winters. A warmer climate could extend the tourist season, allowing more visitors to explore Greenland over a more extended period of the year.

2. **Access to Previously Inaccessible Areas**: Melting ice and snow may render previously inaccessible regions of Greenland open to exploration. This could unveil new hiking trails, vistas, and unique landscapes for tourists.

3. **New Activities**: Warmer temperatures and changing landscapes might introduce new recreational activities. For instance, sea kayaking, fishing in new areas, and even certain watersports might become more popular.

4. **Wildlife Watching**: As marine ecosystems change, there's potential for different marine life to become more visible around Greenland. While this might offer more opportunities for whale and seal watching, it also means that some species

traditional to the region might become less common.

5. **Increased Cruise Tourism**: Melting sea ice, especially in the Northwest Passage, makes Arctic cruising more feasible. Greenland can become a significant stop for Arctic cruises, boosting local economies in port towns.

6. **Cultural Tourism**: A longer tourism season might allow more tourists to engage with Greenland's rich indigenous Inuit culture. This can include participating in festivals, learning about traditional practices, and exploring Greenlandic cuisine.

7. **Infrastructure Development**: Increased tourism can stimulate investments in infrastructure, including hotels, transport facilities, and amenities. This, in turn, can further boost tourism by making travel to and within Greenland more comfortable.

8. **Economic Diversification**: Greenland's economy has historically been reliant on fishing. Tourism presents an opportunity for economic diversification, creating jobs in various sectors from hospitality to guiding services.

However, there are challenges and considerations:

- **Environmental Impact**: Increased tourism can have environmental consequences, especially in a fragile ecosystem like Greenland's. Measures need to be in place to ensure that tourism growth is sustainable and doesn't harm local habitats.

- **Cultural Sensitivity**: It's essential to ensure that tourism respects and preserves the local Inuit culture, avoiding the pitfalls of commercialization or misrepresentation.

- **Over-tourism**: Popular destinations could face the risk of over-tourism, which can strain local resources and negatively impact the experience for both tourists and residents.

- **Climate Unpredictability**: While a warmer climate might open up new opportunities, it also brings unpredictable weather patterns, which can pose challenges for planning and safety.

In conclusion, while a warming climate offers potential for a booming tourism industry in Greenland, careful and thoughtful management is essential to ensure that it benefits both visitors and the local population, all while preserving the natural and cultural treasures of the region.

New shipping routes

The ongoing retreat of Arctic sea ice due to global warming is reshaping maritime navigation. Greenland, given its strategic location in the Arctic, is poised to play a pivotal role as new shipping routes emerge. These changes could have profound implications for global trade, geopolitics, and Greenland's own economic and strategic positioning. Here's how a warmer climate might affect shipping routes related to Greenland:

1. **Northwest Passage**: Historically, the Northwest Passage, which runs through the Canadian Arctic Archipelago, was mostly unnavigable due to thick sea ice. However, diminishing ice coverage is making it increasingly feasible for ships to traverse this route during certain times of the year. This passage offers a shortcut between the North Atlantic and North Pacific, significantly reducing voyage times between Europe and Asia compared to the Panama Canal route.

2. **Northeast Passage (Northern Sea Route)**: While this route lies off the northern coast of Russia and doesn't directly touch Greenland, its increasing feasibility impacts global shipping dynamics. The route offers another shortcut between Europe and Asia, decreasing the transit time compared to the Suez Canal route.

3. **Economic Opportunities for Greenland**: As the Arctic routes become more active, Greenland can capitalize by developing ports, offering refueling and resupplying services, and even setting up search and rescue facilities. This can boost local economies and generate employment.

4. **Shorter Transit Times**: For many shipping routes, especially between Asia and Europe or the eastern coast of North America, the Arctic pathways could offer significantly shorter transit times, leading to cost savings and reduced carbon emissions.

5. **Geopolitical Importance**: The opening of Arctic shipping lanes adds a new dimension to geopolitics. Countries are vying for influence in the Arctic, given its strategic and economic importance. Greenland's position can make it a significant player in Arctic geopolitics.

6. **Environmental Concerns**: Increased shipping in the Arctic comes with significant environmental concerns. The potential for oil spills, disruptions to marine ecosystems, and the impact of increased human activity in a fragile environment are real challenges. Moreover, shipping contributes to black carbon deposits on ice, accelerating melting.

7. **Safety Challenges**: The Arctic, even with reduced ice, is a challenging and unpredictable environment for navigation. Ships need to be ice-strengthened, and there's a need for improved navigation aids, mapping, and satellite communication.

8. **Infrastructure Development**: To support increased shipping activity, there will be a need for infrastructure development in Greenland. This includes ports, repair facilities, and communication systems.

9. **Cultural and Social Impacts**: Increased shipping and related infrastructure development can have impacts on local

communities in Greenland. It's vital to ensure that developments are done in consultation with local communities, respecting their rights and traditions.

10. **Legal and Regulatory Implications**: The legal status of certain Arctic waters, especially the Northwest Passage, is disputed. While Canada views it as internal waters, others see it as an international strait. As traffic increases, there will be a need for clear regulations and agreements to prevent disputes.

11. **Competition with Traditional Routes**: Even with the advantages of shorter transit times, Arctic routes compete with established routes through the Suez and Panama Canals. Factors like seasonality, ice conditions, insurance costs, and vessel types will influence the choice of routes by shipping companies.

In summary, a warmer climate is ushering in a new era for Arctic navigation, with Greenland poised to play a central role. While there are significant opportunities, there are also challenges to ensure sustainable, safe, and equitable development.

Infrastructure development

The impacts of a warmer climate on Greenland are multifaceted, influencing not only its natural environment but also its socio-economic landscape. Infrastructure development is one such area where the effects of climate change can be seen, both in terms of challenges and opportunities:

1. **Ports and Harbors**: As sea ice retreats and new shipping routes open up, there's a need for the development of ports and harbors to support increased maritime activity. These facilities would cater to commercial shipping, fishing fleets, cruise ships, and potentially even naval vessels.

2. **Airports**: The Greenlandic government has been investing in the modernization and expansion of its airport infrastructure.

Warmer climates can increase the length of the operational season and, combined with rising tourism and economic activity, justify further airport developments. Projects like the expansion of Nuuk, Ilulissat, and Qaqortoq airports are examples.

3. **Roads**: As of now, most towns in Greenland aren't connected by roads, and transportation between them primarily relies on boats or aircraft. A warmer climate might facilitate the construction of roads or improve existing road conditions, although the vast distances and challenging terrains would still pose significant obstacles.

4. **Housing and Urban Infrastructure**: As Greenland's economy evolves and potentially diversifies, there might be an influx of people to urban areas. This would necessitate the construction of new housing, public utilities, and other urban infrastructure.

5. **Communications Infrastructure**: Economic growth, increased tourism, and more significant international involvement will demand better communication networks, including expanded internet coverage and more reliable telecommunications systems.

6. **Energy Infrastructure**: Currently, Greenland largely relies on imported oil for energy. As demand grows, there's potential for the development of renewable energy projects, like hydropower or wind energy, necessitating new infrastructure.

7. **Research Facilities**: The Arctic, being at the frontline of climate change, attracts international scientific attention. Upgraded or new research facilities can support global climate studies, glaciology, marine biology, and more.

8. **Search and Rescue Facilities**: Increased maritime activity in Arctic waters necessitates better-equipped search and rescue facilities. This is crucial given the challenging Arctic environment and the potential risks associated with maritime

operations.

9. **Environmental Management Infrastructure**: With increased economic activities, especially in sectors like mining or oil and gas, there's a need for infrastructure to manage waste, treat pollutants, and safeguard the environment.

10. **Challenges to Infrastructure Development**:
    ◦ *Permafrost Thaw*: As the climate warms, permafrost, the permanently frozen ground found in many parts of Greenland, is beginning to thaw. This can lead to ground instability, challenging the construction and maintenance of infrastructure.
    ◦ *Sea Level Rise*: Rising sea levels pose risks to coastal infrastructure, including ports, harbors, and urban centers.
    ◦ *High Costs*: Greenland's remote location, challenging environment, and limited local workforce can make infrastructure development expensive.
    ◦ *Environmental Concerns*: Infrastructure projects need to ensure they don't harm the fragile Arctic environment or disrupt local ecosystems.

In conclusion, a warmer climate presents Greenland with both opportunities and challenges concerning infrastructure development. While there's potential for significant growth and modernization, careful planning is essential to ensure sustainability, cost-effectiveness, and environmental preservation.

Biodiversity changes

The Arctic region, where Greenland is situated, is particularly sensitive to the impacts of climate change. As temperatures rise, the biodiversity of Greenland is undergoing significant alterations. Here's an overview of the biodiversity changes in Greenland due to a warmer climate:

1. **Shift in Range of Species**: As temperatures rise, many species are moving northwards. This shift allows species previously found in more temperate zones to establish themselves in Greenland. For instance, certain bird species, insects, and even fish might expand their ranges northward into Greenlandic territories.

2. **Impact on Marine Life**:
    - *Fish*: Species like Atlantic cod, which had decreased in abundance due to colder waters, are now returning. Mackerel and herring, which were not typically found in Greenlandic waters, are now appearing in increasing numbers.
    - *Marine Mammals*: The reduction of sea ice affects seals and polar bears. Seals use the ice to rest, give birth, and escape predators. Polar bears rely on sea ice to hunt for seals. As ice retreats, these species face challenges related to habitat loss.
    - *Plankton Shifts*: Changes in sea temperatures and ice cover are impacting the composition and distribution of phytoplankton and zooplankton, foundational to the marine food web.

3. **Terrestrial Mammals**: Arctic hare, musk oxen, and caribou are native Greenlandic mammals. Changes in vegetation and habitat due to warming might influence their food availability and migration patterns.

4. **Birdlife**:
    - The nesting patterns of migratory birds might change due to shifts in temperature.
    - New species might begin to nest in Greenland, while some native species might face challenges from altered habitats and increased competition.

5. **Flora**:

- ○ *Shrubification*: Warmer temperatures are leading to the expansion of shrubs in areas that were once dominated by grasses and lichens. This phenomenon, known as "shrubification," can impact the habitat of certain animals and change the soil nutrient cycle.
- ○ *Introduction of New Plant Species*: As the climate becomes milder, it's possible that non-native plant species may establish themselves, potentially competing with native flora.

6. **Insects and Pests**: There's a noticeable increase in certain insect populations, including mosquitoes. Additionally, pests and pathogens previously not found in Greenland might establish themselves, posing threats to native species.

7. **Loss of Ice Habitats**: Many species are specially adapted to life on or around ice. As glaciers and sea ice recede, these species lose their habitats. The melting of ice also releases freshwater into the ocean, which can impact salinity levels and further disrupt marine ecosystems.

8. **Increased Human Interaction**: As the human population grows and activities such as fishing, mining, and tourism expand, there will be more interactions with wildlife. This can lead to challenges related to habitat disturbance, pollution, and potential conflicts with wildlife.

9. **Feedback Loops**: Changes in biodiversity can create feedback loops. For example, the expansion of darker shrubs increases solar radiation absorption, leading to more warming. Similarly, changes in the population of certain species can impact the populations of their predators or prey, leading to cascading effects through the ecosystem.

10. **Conservation Challenges**: As biodiversity changes, there's a need to re-evaluate conservation strategies. Protecting certain species or habitats might require new approaches, and there

might be a need to prioritize based on the degree of vulnerability or the ecological importance of a species.

In conclusion, Greenland's biodiversity is undergoing significant changes due to a warming climate. The intricate interplay between different species and their environments means that small changes can have cascading impacts. While some species might benefit or adapt, others face significant challenges that threaten their survival. Monitoring, research, and adaptive conservation strategies will be critical to navigating these changes.